LOSERS
And Femme Fatales

Manual for
Superior Men

A complete theory based on Einstein physics,
Political Psychology, Systems Theory
and Archetypal Psychiatry.

FORMULA

All success attraction
All disease obstruction
All recovery elimination

You must fast on all three

OBSTRUCTIONS:

People
Habit
Food

LOSERS AND FEMME FATALES

I felt enormous grief from how they treated me. I saw the other side of life: people, evil, strife. A joyful heart is good medicine but the traumatized become ugly as the system spirals down suddenly. They'd project a bad rep on me, act like they owned me, proceed to kill my spirit and take my liberty. Caught in projections without solution I went dead praying God would end it. They had no idea who I was nor could they ever. It was the Dunning-Kruger effect of the unclever.

BROKEN QUEENS

DISLOYALTY TRIGGERS
TRAINED FROM LOSS OF DIGNITY
CHASING INFERIOR MEN
CURE FOR NARCISSISTC ABUSE
HE'S NATURALLY DISLOYAL
ALWAYS SHOOTING HIS SHOT
FRAGILITY OR SENSITIVITY?
RIDDING THE DARK ACCUSATORY PAST
MEGHAN AND HARRY LIBERALS
WIVES VS. THE SILLY WOMEN
STOKED IS RELIGIOUS CONVERSION
PUBLIC SELF-DISCLOSURES
OPEN TO FUTURE/THERE IS NO PAST
SINNERS VS. BEING BOLD
GO FORWARD, THE PAST IS GONE
PHYSICAL REFLECTIONS
SUCCESS IS INEVITABLE

LOSERS
AND
FEMME FATALES

KAREN KELLOCK

THE BROKEN QUEEN

DISLOYALTY TRIGGERS

You sense disloyalty in the environment and like a wild animal dig in/gear up: you don't need this.

Females who don't fit are called Inconvenient Women, burned as witches from the beginning.

Sudden trauma brings moral collapse and then the world flows in to take advantage/give the axe.

The reward for enduring public humiliation [that would make others cave in] is success/renown.

Wife of the alcoholic: they blame her because they don't see how she's being treated in private.

Because he's shallow he's a no-go. He's gonna hurt you girl, flipping the script/discarding ya' know.

Forced conformity crushed me. I felt homesick--terrified, unfree--from the spirit of the groupie.

People get mentally ill just as they do physically ill and it'd be temporary if no [SRIs] meds see.

When the Potter was done he took me outa my cabin and put me into my mansion in the sun.

Solution for PTSD intrusive memories: I Pray God removes all that's not of Him inside of me.

TRAINED FROM LOSS OF DIGNITY

We are trained better by our losses of dignity than anything else. Pride provides the fuse.

BROKEN QUEENS

Suddenly you see you were just one among many. You felt special but it was all a game see.

Suddenly you sense his narcissistic insincerity and it turns you off for good fortunately.

You went back, you relapsed, you forgot. Return to the right path and start again/blot it all out.

If every time you get close you feel revolted, disgusted, hurt and devalued then drop him Sue.

His wife escaped him, never again heard from. See him thru HER eyes and learn fast/volumes.

Stop tracking the mind. Gain insights from stopping all videos and media and just going inside.

I wasn't impressed how he talked and my mother was not. Filthy language belies the ol' sot.

If he talks like that on television what does he do when you're not around him? Just imagine.

Lose your home, lose your freedom because you're only free with a strong boundary see/alone.

Perverted male culture seeks to break a woman. Wreck her resolve, rough her up some, put her down.

CHASING INFERIOR MEN

Don't get involved with that cad, I'm telling you Madge. Didn't all ill advised affairs start with that?

While she's chasing she's missing seasons when she should be planting, watering, harvesting.

The feminine soul needs to be desired, pursued and cherished--this never comes if he's chased.

BROKEN QUEENS

Respect precedes love. Whenever she chases a man respect is off the table and it gets rough.

Every time she chases it tears her core. She needs to be honored yet this is hurting her more.

By needing "love" she's an accomplice to her own broken soul. Queens don't chase/stay home.

Sometimes a heart has to break for the soul to heal. You need to shut it down with that heel.

You must see it as an unequal yoke. If you run him down by chasing you'll always be after the bloke.

Friends follow through, show fidelity, aren't creepy and don't talk behind your back honey.

Once behind a wall you never have to deal with invasive officious users again. Hallelujah, amen!

Message to Champions: Be superior in your selections and you'll be superior in your outcomes.

CURE FOR NARCISSISTC ABUSE

Cure for narcissistic abuse: Put signs up all around that you're number ONE or he can get lost.

For he will discard you for another, that's his main characteristic: fickleness of a hunter.

If he's coming on to you, don't personalize it but see it as his GAME and there are many Sue.

The soul tie is always drawing you back in thoughts. Catch these and see you're just another cog.

She was swept up in a soul tie by his hyper come-on personality until she saw there were MANY.

BROKEN QUEENS

Since you're the best--number ONE--any comparison is devaluing so now you must back away.

Your husband is in love with you only, no wondering eyes. Let this be your barometer/no bad guys.

You eventually get sick of his blatant and fickle insincerity and pull way back, quietly.

Don't forget shallowness is insincerity and insincerity indicates shallowness so he's a mess.

The narcissist sees office conquests as fun and exciting and in marriage he's even more that way.

HE'S NATURALLY DISLOYAL

The narcissist is naturally disloyal. He'll always see the office girls as better looking than his gal.

No wife just ups and leaves without a reason. She saw what you see and it was even worse then.

If he hurts you with narcissistic fickleness he's not your husband that's all-- only way to look at this.

Always look at it as Melania would see it. She'd never chase this bad dream of never coming first.

Be like Trump: just return to your castle and let the hypnotized rabble fight it out, that's all.

You come number ONE or the answer is NO. Put signs up on your walls: NUMBER ONE OR NO.

Don't ever settle for less due to your age etc. You are number ONE no matter how they frame ya.

They frame you and now you say: GO, because you are rude and cruel no matter if it is the truth.

BROKEN QUEENS

For a true narcissist cannot love you as you want and your self-worth is sure to take a plunge.

As the ancient Chinese say, return to the right path and no blame. Be more YOU and much less him.

You allowed the world to break queen consciousness. A broken soul ever seeking to kiss up/a mess.

You shook with adoration before your hero who now turns out to be hurtfully fickle and shallow.

Let the veil fall from your eyes as the hero's dethroned and depedestalized. Honey he's not your guy.

For no one's perfect or that good and you made him something he is not in your thoughts.

ALWAYS SHOOTING HIS SHOT

Life is hell if you're gonna hang your happiness on a pick. He's always shooting his shot, illegit.

He loves seeing the effect his clever hand has on others. Whether girls or youth he's forever clever.

He's too shallow to love you with depth you need girl. And what of commitment? Go forward.

The final goodbye is a silent cut off. It's all been said before you just didn't have the guts.

You know what he's like now and he's not gonna change. He may just get more needy as he ages.

So he wasn't the right one, so what. You didn't make a mistake you just learned about fakes fast.

Now have a nice day, filled with your own thoughts and who YOU are at your best and highest ok.

BROKEN QUEENS

I felt alienated as a groupie. It was social [loyalty to group] not autonomy: we were black sheep.

Think of his wife, what she went through. To understand fickle put yourself in her shoes.

FRAGILITY OR SENSITIVITY?

They call me fragile cuz things affect me that don't affect the rabble, the thick or muscled.

Remember SS: Soy Sequesters. In fat—that's why the protuberances which do NOT attract.

If you eliminate the fat the toxins invade the core and that means death so you can't get rid of it.

To protect the vital organs—heart and lungs—you have strips of fat your exercise can't get off.

Experiment: eat the main candy bars for a few days and watch total load go way up/you're stuck.

For breakfast eat the bakery pastries filled with soy and watch total load go up/looking like a toad.

The warm/sweet/starchy/fatty breakfasts were good for you but now the soy is destroying us Sue.

They said meat would increase immunity but it raised total load so much I caught everything.

And what about the evident kidney dysfunction signaled by eye-bags and bloated lower legs?

I'm not exactly an insomniac I just work all night. I start my day before midnight then it excites.

They make you feel like you've done something horribly wrong or disgusting and that's your identity.

BROKEN QUEENS

Women had license to erupt and erupt they did. I've done it myself, payback for history I guess.

If the only way they can fight/win is to get dirty in court they'll do it/divorce industry pushes it.

Is it true love or a soul tie? Soul ties are sexual as a familiar spirit keeps drawing you back, aye.

A massive soul tie develops when you're degraded and accept it. It's a pathetic thing sucking up.

Soul ties are seeded from early trauma bonds then with sex/hormones made most strong.

They said "delicate health and fragility". Or is it extreme super sensitivity and dying to be free?

RIDDING THE DARK ACCUSATORY PAST

Past is literally gone/never existed cuz God erases it. Only good memories remain in present.

Constant thoughts of self-disgust and shame indicate a generational curse landing on the lonely.

For so many years I was to blame for everything then I was muted/silenced from spilling the beans.

It's a helluva thing when the wife of the alcoholic gets sicker than he as a blamed lunatic raving.

He's the alcoholic but she's blamed for it and, since drinking is the major mal-adaptation, IS it.

Lovestruck can be horrible cuz you're so outa control. You don't even care if it's a tie of the soul.

An event puts you in touch with mortality and your entire view of reality changes suddenly.

BROKEN QUEENS

Children/pets are victims of adult vacillation, insecurity, neuroses and fuddyduddiness.

MEGHAN AND HARRY LIBERALS

Meghan and Harry signed the deals to dish the dirt. They did it, no going back, now the hurt.

Harry's book is full of narcissism, revenge, betrayal and white trash vulgarity. Jared Taylor

Of course Meghan's behind it. Women mold men's minds and sex has much to do with it.

Men should rule but in this generation they listen to the women or fake agreement with them.

Conservative females don't take it personally, knowing the truth about most women presently.

We've stopped arguing with sisters in TDS syndrome, calling Trump "most evil and despicable."

Liberals have hated/wanted to destroy America since the sixties. This is just the culmination see.

They're very angry about it too, madly deluded. They get together and rev it up/so dangerous.

They're so self righteous signaling virtuous I don't see how their husbands stand the broads.

Payoff: to continue his sex supply the husband goes along with his wife so hypnotized and silly.

WIVES VS. THE SILLY WOMEN

The wives are watching CNN/nbc which doesn't even show the border crises, don't you see.

BROKEN QUEENS

These main media are arms of the dems and gophers for Biden. Only silly women listen to em.

Bible calls em silly women for good reason: easy for wicked men to creep in and hypnotize em.

They listen to the paid stooges calling themselves journalists. It's the prostitute media sis.

Hang around those people and your head's in a dungeon. Low self-esteem sets in--avoid em.

Meghan'll have a book too. It's the royal couple, a legend to themselves telling of the feud.

Sure of their position as all liberals are, tho' their insides are shaky because they're so wrong.

In this era of malevolent egalitarianism we see *most* racism tho' it's veiled by progressivism.

STOKED IS RELIGIOUS CONVERSION

Harry has undergone RELIGIOUS CONVERSION. That's what love and sex does I'm afraid son.

LOVE: It's overwhelming, it consumes the mind, it's mind-transporting, it overtakes you, aye.

Meghan's his priestess bringing him into the absurd California therapy culture of Me First.

Feelings more than facts, "my truth" since everything is relative, the whole bag is self-destructive.

He contradicts himself cuz the religious conversion isn't complete--back and forth but can't see it.

The new gospel of Woke and Mental Wellbeing is pure heresy and it's destroyed Harry see.

17

BROKEN QUEENS

PUBLIC SELF-DISCLOSURES

Diana started the tradition of public self-disclosure so Harry continued it cuz it worked before.

Hope delivers a better future but bitterness only despair. Forgive em and let go/have flair.

They're selling us dystopia. They're selling us depression. Above all, avoid their medications.

Sensitivity sux. Every little thing makes you sick: in a bubble and having constantly to adjust.

They tell us we're going into a better world but it's just a trap and a black hole. Fight back/be bold.

OPEN TO FUTURE/THERE IS NO PAST

Open to future, there is no past. This is Einstein information/it's just a dimension, have a blast.

Some get meaner with age, others get calmer, nicer, gentler cuz they've seen how life can change.

The saints have a stinging conscience and it gets so bad remorse is a major block to get rid of.

We did it, we own it and we repent. Now get rid of it: Paul said that was his major achievement.

Jesus died so we could be free of the darkness of sin. What is this but memory? Be free then.

You can waste your life watching infinite videos. Why them? Think about it man, avoid grooves.

When men come outa haze of promiscuity or women the haze of pugnacity, there's much to face.

SINNERS VS. BEING BOLD

BROKEN QUEENS

They want to boldly declare these truths themselves but lack the Christian constraint it takes.

You can't just be audacious for the sake of audacity but temper it with humility: that's how to be.

To escape him/her was the greatest relief in life. People are dangerous and filled with strife.

It is our losses of dignity that teach us better than anything else. it's like a milestone sis.

Public humiliation provides fodder for making gold, giving intense heat to transmute the old.

Think of a ghost town. Do we remember all the things happening in the long past there? NONE.

GO FORWARD, THE PAST IS GONE

God says go forward, the foe is dead or gone. The time is late/there's nothing stopping you now.

He says he's changed but his words belie he hasn't. He's the same so drop him from your spirit.

They're rubbing bumbling Biden out. He'll either resign or say he'll not be running again, caio.

Here's how you tell a narcissist: As soon as you lay a boundary he busts it. He can't stand it!

The etiology of anorexia is a comment someone made. The hypersensitive heard it and caved.

I fuel the tank at dawn, I pull the bands later on, I enjoy the view as perception reveals ALL.

See the difference between shortbread [flour sugar butter] and adulterated/poisoned others.

BROKEN QUEENS

Anorexia has a new category: those who don't eat to prevent acid reflux/choking in their sleep.

Women love bakery--pies, cookies and cakes--but since they slipped in soy it destroyed their looks.

There's also micro-evolution: the changes reflecting dietary habits as daily routines son.

PHYSICAL REFLECTIONS

She was so depleted/sick of being cheated her skin just hung on her, her psychology reversed.

Eat at dawn, exercise in afternoon. Fasting with exercise evokes HGH: human growth hormone.

Pull those bands, the muscles tend to atrophy and the skin shrivels up too see. Pull: 1 - 2 - 3...

Jet pills are not caffeine, there's some chemical in there and I'll never take one again I swear.

Is it anorexia or fastarian consciousness? A wanna be, an aspirant to the highest of the galaxy see.

Even the unvaxxed are dropping dead from heart attacks just like the bible said of the last.

In California the cost of building a new house is 1/3 permit fees. Overregulation treachery.

Demographic change [mass replacement] hurts like hell as your piece of the pie dwindles to nil.

If we're not safe we're not sovereign, period. If a sense of security is trashed we're powerless.

Big ones of 2023: anti-immigration, anti-establishment, anti-war and anti-tax. Gerald Cilante

BROKEN QUEENS

SUCCESS IS INEVITABLE

You've reached a perfect plateau to review all your work. See the whole so it comes first.

God knew that them putting me down would fire ambition in me like you've never known.

Don't worry about success, it'll find you fast. Just prepare for the new life, that's the gist.

Start your weekends on Wednesday. You won't believe what that does for your creativity ok.

LOSERS

AVOID MERRY GO ROUNDS
JEALOUS GRUNTS
PRESSURED BY PRECEDENTS
THE INEVITABLE DISCARD
PERVERSION OF BIRDS AND BEES
DELILAHS AND SVENGALIS
INTENTIONAL SEX ADDICTION
SWEET SUGAR AVOIDS INTIMACY
STIGMA
AS THE GENERATIONS PASS
CONTROL THRU SMEAR FEARS
MAKING SENSE IN A DUMBED WORLD
MERCILESS HEATHEN
DEATH OF MEMORY
UNSAFE TO DEVIATE
HEEDING THE SENSE OF DANGER
TRAINED TO SUCK IT UP
APERTURE SYNDROME
NEVER COMPARE YOURSELF
DON'T COMPLAIN
DON'T COMPETE
HIX POLITIX
TOXIC FEMALE FRIENDS
GOOD FRIENDS ARE MATURE
FEMALE COMMUNITY VS. GENIUS
FEMALES AND FLYING MONKEYS
SUDDEN GHOSTING
CASUAL SEX AND KARMA
FEMALE FRENEMIES

LOSERS

PRACTICE VACUITY
BE HAPPILY ALONE
CLEAN A DRAWER: DUMP IT OUT
DISCONNECTED: NO ONE KNEW ME
EMOTIOANLLY ABANDONNED
NARCISSISTIC APATHY AND OBLIVION
SOCIOPATHIC NARCISSISM
DAMAGING ELEMENTS, ALWAYS
YOU'RE JUST WORN OUT
BLURRY BOUNDARIES HURT THE MOST
HEALTH-DRAINING RELATIONSHIPS
LIVING WITH A RATTLESNAKE
I WAS NICE AFTER ALL
REGAIN YOUR BOUNDARIES NOW
LEFTIST OBLIVIOUS LOSERS
PROTESTS AND LOOTING
AGENDA: TO DESTROY SOCIETY
WHEN THEY WAKE UP THEY WON'T BELIEVE IT
THEY'RE AGING BABIES
ADDICTED: EMPTY SHELLS
PROTECTION, PROVISION, EXPANSION
MARRIAGE IS FREEDOM FOR FEMALES
BEHIND A FENCE YOU EXPAND!
NO MORE IDENTITY POLITICS!
EMOTIONAL INDOCTRINATIONS
CURE FOR LOSERS: BECOME FASTERS
EATING BECOMES IRRELEVANT/A CHORE
WE'RE WOUNDED CHILDREN
FENCED OFF FROM THE MOB
GO EMPTY SO GOD WILL FILL
MY OWN BORDERS

LOSERS

DISTRACTIONS VS. SOLITUDE
GENIUS DOESN'T FIT, CHAMELEONS AREN'T LEGIT
POPULAR APPROVAL SEALS THEIR DEMISE
RUTHLESS GOSSIPS AND TALEBARERS
CREATE A SPACE: BYE-BYE BABY
DEMONIC FORCES IN POLITIX
NOXIOUS EVENTS ARE JUST TRAINING
HYPERSEXUALIZED TEEN WORLD
LIBERAL NIGHTMARE: SELECTIVE BLINDNESS
SOCIAL DOESN'T MEAN RELIGIOUS
EMERGENT CHURCH COMFORTS SINNERS
MEMORY STORED IN SHIT
THEY EFFECT US LIKE DOWNERS
HYPERSENSITIVES READ THOUGHTS: OUCH
DELAY BETWEEN PLANTING AND HARVESTING
LIONS REJECT OPINIONS OF SHEEP
CAPTURED LEFTIST CHURCHES
FASCINATION OF YOUR OWN MIND
PUNISHED BY THEIR PRESENCE
SEEKING SOLITUDE CAN BE DANGEROUS
WOMEN CONTROL THROUGH GOSSIP AND OSTRACISM
DANGEROUS HIX POLITIX
JEZEBEL SPIRIT DESTROYS YOUR SELF WILL
LADY PREACHERS
AUTOIMMUNE DIET FOR THE SENSITIVE
OLD LADY DIET: SMOOTHIES, SOUPS, SALAD, DIPS
NO TRIGGERED IMMUNE: FRUIT/SALADS
VICTORY IN DARKNESS: THIS BJ THING
TWO-SPEED LIFE: TUNNEL-VISION VS. RELAX
DEEP THROAT AND THE ENDLESS CONTRACT
LEISURE EVOKES GENIUS
WATCH OUT FOR WOMEN
BIG EGOS GOTTA GO

Preface
THE SYSTEM

AVOID MERRY GO ROUNDS

What to tell your daughters: Avoid the merry go round of a fast ride bringing you to nothing, ever.

A fast ride is thrilling, dizzying but redundant. A flashy car going nowhere and besides he's a nut.

Being trapped in going-nowhere relationships can be dangerous as your life is on the line sis.

It starts with lovebombing, demonstrations of love and affection which to the broken are overwhelming.

A man who flatters his neighbor spreads a net for his feet--bad marriages always start good see.

A net under his feet: he can't run or even walk, he falls. He soaks it up from prior trauma long ago.

JEALOUS GRUNTS

Her sisters were jealous bully grunts and her mother was a narcissistic sadist, a progressive drunk.

Tell me a sad girl from that background won't suck it up when flattered or mercilessly lovebombed.

Flatter is a net under his feet: he "falls" in love, hopelessly though temporarily defeated.

Loveboming is satanically designed to make the victim FALL IN LOVE. It's a trap of the velvet glove.

LOSERS and Femme Fatales

He got her so carried away emotionally she didn't have time to think--all it took was his smile or wink.

It's like a sudden whirlwind happening so fast she's stunned, locked into place, mesmerized.

It's healthy to walk into love with eyes wide open after a time of probation not fall into a maelstrom.

Before she knows it she's fallen in love with one sent directly from the devil but acts like a dove.

They smother you/don't give you a chance to think. They occupy all your time/wrong seems so right.

PRESSURED BY PRECEDENTS

She always prayed for someone to love her like this and here comes another dozen roses sis.

You've done all this but now feel so pressured by precedent as they've grown to expect it.

How can you resist this? By getting hep and realizing this person is just setting you up for a diss.

Don't argue with em just flush em out. These are litmus tests of character: take note then avoid all.

Watch others who create temptations or obstacles. Turn away from their appetites/base desires.

Through smooth/flattering speech they deceive the hearts of the unsuspecting, innocent and naive.

The wise and mature aren't captivated by fake sweet but just want the loyal and consistent see.

Slow down. You've got nothing to prove to me and I get nervous with this shameless show see.

LOSERS and Femme Fatales

Women do it too: spread their net so the man falls in love and it's all about sex not from above.

THE INEVITABLE DISCARD

When you're where they want you the whole game changes: roses stop, calls too, broken pledges.

When they start at dessert or offer to refinish all your furniture first they change fast/empty flirts.

They start with the ice cream and sweets but there's no significance, no depth--but not to the naive.

You get sick of the sweets fast and start looking around for steaks. They're empty nutrition and fakes.

Try not to relive the past because you can't afford the adrenalin rush: conserve your energy sis.

A queen is never lovebombed and discarded. Recall these two go together and march forward.

With a king yes is yes and no is no, there are no games the queen has to wade thru and she glows.

Despite the urgent lovebombing and wild sex she realizes: there's no intimacy, no real significance.

PERVERSION OF BIRDS AND BEES

This is perversion of the natural: the birds and bees. It's all backward and manipulative you see.

Sex, sex and more sex with someone who is emotionally unavailable and unsubstantial as a fairy tale.

It's quite a discovery that they give you their body but never access to their soul or heart/EMPTY.

LOSERS and Femme Fatales

He knows how to make her respond physically but does nothing for her soul or mind: runs on EMPTY.

He addicts and hypnotizes her thru sex as she enters a dark mental cavern of his demonic hex.

DELILAHS AND SVENGALIS

A sex addict loses the mind and selectively disattends from things they should be focusing on.

Both sexes to it: there are Delilahs and Svengalis. This is why it's best to avoid it all through chastity. START START

He addicts her to lovebombing and when she needs more than sex, roses & candy he leaves her hanging.

He gives just enough to keep the system going but it's all fluff and when done he's gone again.

They overload you with compliments but never really invest in the relationship in great depth.

Roses and flattery are cheap but depth and intimacy bringing satisfaction takes time investment see.

He lovebombed her all the way to the altar and later she realized that he had no depth whatsoever.

INTENTIONAL SEX ADDICTION

Women are sex addicts like men who hypnotize them thru their sexual instincts –then she loses it.

She married a narcissist who used her for his own purposes and is still using her in marriage.

Now we're in phase two where you're always left hanging: an itch you can't scratch see.

LOSERS and Femme Fatales

If people are in your life you likely take their advice and when it goes repeatedly wrong, bye bye.

Bad advice of frenemies is so expensive you finally learn your lesson and it's good riddance see.

It's all good but there's something missing. They know how to have sex but there's no love making.

A narcissist has no self-awareness nor inclination to go inner so there's nothing to give to her.

SWEET SUGAR AVOIDS INTIMACY

Too much sugar makes you sick and angry at the empty calories when there's no superfood see.

They know how to have sex but have no conversation nor any idea who you are internally son.

There's a total disconnect spiritually, emotionally and intellectually. They do not know you honey.

An intimacy avoider won't engage deep conversations or or ever agree to talk about their "feelings".

They will find their way out of all heart conversations. They have no time for them as irrelevant.

A cookie cutter answer then slide right out of it. No response to a painful truth questioning it.

You pour your heart out and without any empathy or connection they can't handle it, evasion.

You talk of your goals and aspirations and they can't relate. It's just too intimate so they escape.

They're never comfortable in silence, marking intimacy. They always end up with small talking.

LOSERS and Femme Fatales

Her spirit's stronger than her lows/highs, her creativity outshines day/night but not with that guy.

THEY CAN'T STAND SILENCE

They gotta turn a radio on or talk about petty stuff and it's aggravating--you're starting to miss depth.

They can't stand silence cuz they can't connect intimately so fill it with the chatty and empty.

Look deep before you leap. THESE are the things to be discovered before going too far my sweet.

Does this person desire to be intimate, does he even have the capacity or will he face judgement?

Sex is not intimacy which goes deeper than surface stuff. Love nevers gives up and is consistent.

Sex is not intimacy which goes deeper than surface stuff. Love is consistent and never gives up.

The greatest gift a man can ever give a woman is consistency or it's emotional treachery.

He deprives her of intimacy and abuses her emotionally making her believe she imagines it all see.

As she comes back to common sense he makes her doubt herself and gaslighting is the result.

Then they make you doubt what you feel and don't feel. You're just a whiny complainer out of keel.

STIGMA

Black sheep is the story of STIGMA. Once pegged the whole town gangs up and it's the end of ya.

LOSERS and Femme Fatales

Once pegged they all point at you, it scratches an itch--but once you're gone you're just a glitch.

If extreme you're more of a legend than a memory, embellished as they will of lost history.

AS THE GENERATIONS PASS

If you'll be forgotten after two generations why be so concerned with what they think now hon'.

Scapegoated by entire town of bloodthirsty bored clowns you think you're the worst ever known.

Don't air dirty laundry cuz they don't know how bad it was and could see it in a good light/blessed.

Not only will mistakes not be remembered, you won't be either so forget it all and just learn.

You're in the Nigredo stage of making gold that's all--where you feel no one's as bad as you, aw.

Was it that you were awful, or their shock at your behavior due to it being so unique/novel?

Recognizing past mental illness is also wildly revealing and embarrassing: when we knew nothing.

Is it how you remember it, or how the Lord remembers it--when he's buried it at bottom of ocean?

Ok so you screwed up cuz you had a demon in you, on the wide path for a time but got off, whew.

He started to drink again and became a totally different person--my bloody worst enemy in my home.

CONTROL THRU SMEAR FEARS

LOSERS and Femme Fatales

The narcissist bullies you through fear of his smear campaigns should you escape his terror.

Smear campaigns: the automatic go-to for the female narcissist should you reject her or diss.

Like lighting a fire, suddenly everyone hates you due to a smear campaign put in the grapevine.

Calumny--destroying your good rep--is tantamount to soul murder and God'll get em quick.

MAKING SENSE IN A DUMBED WORLD

You're trying to make sense of yourself in a dumbed world. Contorting yourself to fit, you warped.

Separate out the truth about you vs. how they pegged you. So often we obsequiously take their view.

You slept in the mud when you fought a war but why sink in your mental swill thereafter?

The more traumatized a girl is by her father the more she's fodder for whatever comes after.

Because they don't like hearing it they say it's false. They even get violent so watch yourself.

Older women mean to younger women: they become mama and if you're unique they hatecha.

She screamed and barked at me. On that day i decided never to get in a car with a harridan again see.

Look at rejection as the greatest thing ever happening to you saving you lotsa trouble too.

As they collude together against her she falls into her bag of anxiety-avoidance coping methods.

LOSERS and Femme Fatales

Who colludes against her? The kings and queens of the earth, the virtue signalers/social manipulators.

To be so stupid as to be trapped in a house or car with someone--oh no no, no more of that hon'.

MERCILESS HEATHEN

There's no mercy with them so stay away. The mere contact spoils/don't give em any energy.

I was always accused you know but sacred cows can do anything and remain above reproach.

It took years and experience to know what you don't want. It's the most important or forget it.

Mom, I'm still mad you spat on my rep. Karen, I'm eternally grateful to you making me hep.

Wishing you were dead is also a result of introjections from a dumb crowd, family/neighborhood.

Adapting to the Dunning-Kruger effect [of dumb in control] has disastrous effects for the Elect.

Forgive yourself for the demon that was in you. It's really weird but it really was the devil who...

DEATH OF MEMORY

When we die all memory is gone. What remains are legends handed down--so why not now?

Why not now have all memory gone? These are anchors of low self-esteem and the devil's song.

Memory-anchors/sin markers disperse as vapors when we die so why not now/there is no past-ers.

LOSERS and Femme Fatales

The past is a lower dimension/I'd hate to mention it. Life is a ladder, you're on top now so forget it.

It was dangerous living in a liberal town of constant vendettas and shifting alliances gossip-run.

If you thought differently they'd bomb your mailbox or do other outrageous things like with Kellock.

UNSAFE TO DEVIATE

It wasn't safe to deviate in anyway or to show yourself as disagreeing with the common view today.

In this dumbed down desolate drought I was a stranger in a strange land/had to find God.

The drought was mental but also emotional as their callous disregard made them feel entitled.

You were punished for being hateful/antisocial for not letting em in/turning your life upside down.

They take no account for danger/don't see a threat. This blase liberal attitude is cultural death.

In a small liberal dumbed down town one word swings em into combat mode and a black cloud.

They selectively disattended from husband's sins only focusing on mine/got everyone agreein'

In cowboy/flyover country no one cares, they're all in their complex households, focus is inner.

HEEDING THE SENSE OF DANGER

Must heed/not silence the feeling of danger around someone you know or a stranger: be aware.

LOSERS and Femme Fatales

I got so used to things not going right nor smoothly I expected only ruin yet fought against it.

Listen: If someone scares you half to death never truckle or sink in your swill but call the sheriff.

I expected only disaster but then recalled: Lord prepared a mansion and wanted me to prosper!

There's no reason everything can't go right now that you're on top having overcome your flop.

TRAINED TO SUCK IT UP

Trained to suck it up and suddenly your life falls apart and what do you do? Drive it in to ruin.

They think as One Mind. that's what makes it so dam frightening, like a bulldozer coming thru, aye.

Let's judge people on two things: their track record and fruits--who they hurt/what they produced.

Sarcasm is condescension. Some people are coarser, some are more sensitive so careful son.

A pool of thirsty options makes em cocky. They have a real edge when everyone wants em see.

You're in for a rude awakening kid: world, family, churches, schools and workplaces are toxic.

As the times get darker all these previously safe places are toxic and even the schools have killers.

As times get darker God reveals Himself more in it. He works from the inside out in our spirit.

My soul--intellect, emotions, personality--was so damaged only thru God's spirit was it salvaged.

LOSERS and Femme Fatales

APERTURE SYNDROME

I was devastated, alone in the desert. I turned to God and felt enlightened, elated and alert.

Ever since I had this psychic opening [aperture syndrome] I was never again bored nor lonely.

It was such a clear life milestone, as everything paled compared to this revelation of the ONE.

Since then people are on probation with me cuz I know I can call on God and His clever creativity.

Aperture Syndrome: there's an opening and all needed info rushes in, no denying it: it's cosmic.

Neurosis and all mental illness is blinders while an opening is awareness of frenemy fakers.

The psychotic is so enmeshed in a sick family system he can't see it: an opening makes it evident.

We were blind, searching in dark for what we could never find. Now we go within to gold, refined.

NEVER COMPARE YOURSELF

Now to stay emotionally healthy, three things: never compare yourself for any reason on anything.

Be careful: Society so diminishes our self-perspective we can never live up to our godly potential.

The result of this early capping of godliness is broken consciousness: looking outside ourselves.

Due to brokenness we're always comparing ourselves: women on body types and men on wallets.

LOSERS and Femme Fatales

Never really happy/content with what God has blessed YOU with and you can't scratch this itch.

Much self-disgust comes from comparisons to the world or seeing self thru it's eyes, an endless grill.

Your looking at a contrived standard outside self and the result is embarrassment, shame, guilt.

Bible calls it unwise to compare yourself. The only standard should be the Lord not outer fluff.

DON'T COMPLAIN

The Lord brings prosperity, going deeper than your address: it's actually living out your purpose.

Does my life please God? Am I fulfilled? Does the way I live elevate others? This is prospering sir.

If my life isn't a blessing to others I'm not truly prosperous. It's a legacy your leaving sis.

You think your life is as bad as it could ever be but then war/deprivation makes you grateful see.

Reality is: your life could be so much worse. Gratitude is the key so keep this realization first.

If you really know how low life can go you come back to your situation and praise God, isn't it so?

People get a false gauge on reality so what they call horrible suffering is really privilege see.

The truly privileged are so far removed they can't even fathom low living when encountering it.

The Israelites walked in circles for 40 years due to complaining--negativity blocks succeeding.

LOSERS and Femme Fatales

Death and life are in the power of the tongue: speak death get death/speak life get life in sum.

Complaining is a waste and counterproductive. If you just live thru it life takes off like a rocket.

DON'T COMPETE

Don't compete. Don't feel like you must outdo someone else, compete only with your higher self.

When you finally stop all comparing, complaining and competing you're no longer envying.

Essence of Christianity is the individual's relation to God. There is no competition/we're all flawed.

What distinguishes queens/kings is they can celebrate achievements cuz there is no competition.

The average woman is always comparing, jealous and thus hateful as is society and the devil.

Silly women are always competing with queens but queens are in competition with no one see.

Queens just manifest the best version of themselves, the average compare/compete until hell.

Could it be the one you compete with is ideally the one you should be learning from? Yes/it's fun.

The person you compete with is supposed to mentor you but he can't since you're jealous too.

I have to find a place of stability and rest cuz I'm living in a storm of upset but God's an individualist.

As you modify a tendency to these things you'll finally have balance & contentment: being free.

LOSERS and Femme Fatales

Enjoy your days while here not relics of the past cuz when you die it vaporizes into emptiness.

If you've worked all your life you may deserve fame and fortune, far above masses holding you down.

HIX POLITIX

Use of the word "billionaire" as a pejorative is morally wrong and dumb. To AOC from Musk.

The 2nd amendment is the only thing keeping this country from becoming China. Royce White

Half of America doesn't know about China and the other half would love us to be China.

They're down on guns but soft on crime. How then can we defend ourselves all day and night?

Millions pouring in--many in combat attire--and to liberals it's a good thing or doesn't seem to matter.

LOSERS

And Femme Fatales

TOXIC FEMALE FRIENDS

I just got along better with males I thought. Women were intimidating, deceptive, easily bought.

Toxic friends give praises to your face then stab you in the back--their own friends hate you in fact.

They say nice things in front of you but what is said behind your back would blow your mind Sue.

They gossip about everything they know but to you they're syrupy sweet, helpful, a sugar coat.

They're cruel, bitter, saying only things you want to hear. Then they get on the horn to smear.

You're in an intense chat, a happy gab then they ghost you and bash your rep behind your back.

Fake friends are dishonest, saying what you want to hear but pushing bad decisions & consequences.

Toxic friends have weak morals. When you're wrong should you take responsibility? They say no.

GOOD FRIENDS ARE MATURE

Good friends are mature and responsible, guiding you on the right path or where you should go.

A friend listens carefully and the conversations are deep but a fake goes off topic or looks away.

40

LOSERS and Femme Fatales

The fake friend frustrates or won't respond to you. It's as if only what she thinks is of any value.

With a false friend you never go deep. She doesn't respond to your feelings but what she thinks.

Cindy was so nurturing/seemed to be listening but then she'd get on the phone and tell everything.

I got really hurt by friend Cindy as she turned the whole town against me while also consoling me.

The female community is a massive impediment to female genius. Learn that, have success.

FEMALE COMMUNITY VS. GENIUS

The female genius becomes overly dependent on her husband and is always needing consoling.

You can't talk to a female about dubious women friends or its blasphemy against all women see.

Do they respond about your problems? Are they patient and empathic or bored and indifferent?

I saw the computer as an enemy since that's where I felt the female treachery--I became homey.

Could women ever trust female friends? Historically yes, at least more than now with evil feminism.

Their mothers were jealous feminists so lacking encouragement they were inferior friends.

Their fathers were absent/indifferent so lacking confirmation how can they confirm you hon'.

Inferior female friendships mark an adulterous generation of broken families and treachery.

LOSERS and Femme Fatales

Frenemies are reckless/immature, dangerously involving you in uncomfortable situations you abhor.

FEMALES AND FLYING MONKEYS

One especially toxic Jezebel would always bring an army with her and I'd feel demolished afterward.

They slice/dice/filet you as they attack. They're particularly good at that as husbands attest.

Any novel idea or remark sends them into a tizzy that you said something so obviously crazy.

They're angry with novelty and try to get their husbands committed for seeing things globally.

If the shrew is angry with you she restricts kids and relatives from your influence, to eschew.

This was an era when misjudgements and smears were so heavy I just had to wait or relocate.

SUDDEN GHOSTING

It's always a horrible feeling with their ghosting, leaving me reeling: "what did I do sweetie?"

Inferior friendships are flaky, there is no sure footing and they can be gone at any time see.

When you're mentally ill does she rush you to recover as fast as possible or patiently wait at all?

With your success they celebrate and when you're grieving they're a wonderful comfort ok?

Good friends defend your name when absent and encourage an image of goodness not bad.

LOSERS and Femme Fatales

There are some females acting super-nurturing or as therapist but they usually flake out too sis.

The answer is to be the kind of woman a man can love and provide a home for. Pets and a fence.

With a good marriage you're now queen of your own domain. Now you choose very carefully ok.

Now I know why women hate women: they too have been burned many times, it toughens.

With feminism these cruel witches are meaner than ever and go to war right off as you cower.

You don't need more of this sweetie. Just be a nice little lady and love your new home and family.

CASUAL SEX AND KARMA

Toxic friends involve you in things you regret later on. It's so bad I still have PTSD today hon'.

An evil friend will encourage an affair or you getting drunk in an unsafe environment I declare.

An evil friend will put down your husband too. She doesn't want you happily protected Sue.

Does she put you in situations where you must lie about? That's a sure sign to get her out.

Casual sex is no karma free crime. To be one with a hussy ruins your plans and makes ya ugly.

Casual pickup sex coarsens a person. He loses his fineness and personal charisma, dumbed.

How could he not lose the fine finesse of character, it's now merged with spirits from the gutter.

LOSERS and Femme Fatales

What a shame: a player needs mob attention for sex addiction which runs him into the ground.

FEMALE FRENEMIES

You tried to flush her out and she didn't pass the test, that's all. Don't think beyond that doll.

Female frenemies: Even the ones in agreement will exhibit those markers, proving you right.

They'll agree women compete/reverse but then do it themselves. What a confused universe.

The tough feminist type is frightening to be around. Scarry, a harridan—a deep DARK cavern.

Treat yourself to movies [mental transport] through time and space to transcend hate/disgrace.

They were all alike though they said they weren't. They said they understood but what a curse.

You made me so crazy I'm just gonna watch movies and wipe you out completely/retrieve destiny.

PRACTICE VACUITY

Empty out the head: practice vacuity Unsub from all those details and just do music/movies.

Stop the inner voices, empty your head [of everyone you know] then put just a few back instead.

The thing aging us fastest is people then substances and then the stress from the first two.

You flushed em out with a test & they flunked it fast so now don't feel bad when you reject sis.

LOSERS and Femme Fatales

People problems: wipe the slate clean. Do it daily if you have to then choose the good not mean.

BE HAPPILY ALONE

At your level the possibility of finding a friend you can trust and relate to are nil, so be still.

They'll go just so far with you then one word turns em away suddenly and they're gone see.

Take no heed when left alone again for that's our escape, new growth seed and regimen.

Suddenly your new friend makes you sick. We overlook things at first then we don't and it clicks.

When you're in my life you're in my head--when that's sad/bad it's gonna be goodbye instead.

Weed your friendship garden like you clean out a drawer: empty out then pick for rapport.

I felt much better after weeding my friendships: like a cool breeze, a brand new start, the epic.

CLEAN A DRAWER: DUMP IT OUT

How to clean a drawer: Dump the whole thing out and penuriously choose back now its fresher.

Make a switch, shave your head, weed your friendships and start a wonderful new life as a kid.

Become a birdwatcher, a walk-for-peacer, a cook and banquet giver, a visionary with a prayer.

Do whatever you have to go within, leave the world out & drill down to the CORE of who you are.

LOSERS and Femme Fatales

I started my new life as a kid with a ten day water fast. Miracles abounded and I came first not last.

What is my found destiny: Open mind, look out the window and write what comes through see.

Magnanimously accept you were robbed then it's holes in their bucket while you're doubled by God.

Get good at starting a new life. Become excellent at it and welcome opportunity to practice it.

DISCONNECTED: NO ONE KNEW ME

I was a woman acquainted with enormous grief. From how they treated me/wouldn't let me be.

They'd project their notions on me, act like they owned me, proceed to kill my spirit/take my liberty.

Caught in their projections without solution I just went dead and prayed God would soon end it.

They had no idea who I was nor could they ever. It was the Dunning-Kruger effect of the unclever.

At least I saw the other side of life, it gave me something to write about: people, evil, strife.

A joyful heart is good medicine but a crushed spirit dries up the bones. And skin, insights, ideas, goals.

The abused traumatized woman starts to look ugly. Now the system spirals down suddenly.

EMOTIOANLLY ABANDONNED

Now I wanna speak about your kin. They're holding you back but you keep hanging on, abandoned.

LOSERS and Femme Fatales

Those people made me sick. You see I didn't know how to deal with it, the weird projections and shit.

I didn't know how to control my homesick emotions in the face of their projections, Lord help me.

They literally made me so sick I made myself sick to mal-adapt cuz I guess that's all I had.

We deal with situations with the tools had at the time and I had none but fearful regressing.

NARCISSISTIC APATHY AND OBLIVION

He is clueless, oblivious to you. There is no meeting of minds but he's emotionally triggered too.

If you trigger him emotionally it overrides anything you can say but he's oblivious to you usually.

He can't parse out nuance: it's his way or no way, black and white thinking, anything else is nuisance.

Any discussion of fine differences meets "I don't need you to teach me anything, I know it all see."

Any calibration of reality--better, best, worst--is met with frustration and irritation/he stays dumb.

Since narcissists are driven by apathy and egotism it's not a good outcome only your frustration.

When with this oblivious clueless narcissist you can only engage functionally: pass the salt see.

It's sad when you want heart connection but they don't do that, it's only what you do for me chap.

Don't expect him ever do understand or care why you do what you do. Silly woman it's him not you.

LOSERS and Femme Fatales

SOCIOPATHIC NARCISSISM

There's no fixing rep in a small town after his smear campaign: shit on the shoe never goes away.

If you're engaged with narcissists they are toxic people and it's just that simple: double trouble.

You can never win and there's gonna be a smear campaign which means incredible pain.

It's ok when a mental slave but when you want out it's total trouble when you try to escape.

It's important to know the toxins--POISONS--remaining in your system after being with a crazy man.

DAMAGING ELEMENTS, ALWAYS

There are elements they bring to your relationship that truly are damaging. Let's look at these.

When one's highly controlling that is NOT an uplifting ingredient but that's how he brings it.

Or what of his self-impressed notion: stepping over you to elevate himself is damaging to self-lovin'

They have very low empathy with a low priority of connecting. It's a sad thing and debilitating.

They just wanna use and exploit, they're superior to you on every point and easily get outa joint.

Constantly living behind a false front, very defensive: all of that is corrosive tho' you don't know it.

Walking on eggshells toxin: guarded, measured, careful what you say cuz you don't wanna upset him.

LOSERS and Femme Fatales

Eggshell anxiety destroys spontaneity: afraid to be me because the last time it wasn't safe see.

Emotional suppression: Despite so many things you'd love to discuss, well...never mind I guess.

You'd love to discuss, parse nuances, discern differences but he NEVER responds to this.

You have all these emotions you're carrying/holding in, creating a buildup of more stress and strain.

Result of ongoing suppression of self and one's real emotions: anxiety, bitterness, depression.

Emotional suppression totally depletes one of his sense of openness, spontaneity, loving being me.

The narc poison depletes your authenticity as you tell people all is ok, covering over his duplicity.

YOU'RE JUST WORN OUT

These things you gotta put up with daily wears you out. You start to look ugly when he shouts.

The worst poison is busted boundaries. He'd let people in when I wanted total and complete privacy.

He steps all over what your opinions or preferences are. Your ways of doing things he disregards.

Establish your own uniqueness, he snuffs that right out. We call this blurry boundaries and it's rough.

You feel ignored, overridden, falsely accused, talked about as if you're not in the room.

You get argumentative, react to them, bring out worst, codependent relapse, busted boundaries.

LOSERS and Femme Fatales

You get argumentative, bring out the worst, busted boundaries, codependent relapse.

How you do things, think, what you love or what stinks: these are your boundaries, gone in a blink!

It's your boundaries you regain when you snatch yourself outa this matrix and RELOCATE.

BLURRY BOUNDARIES HURT THE MOST

He doesn't care what you feel or think and he says that right to your face. You don't matter Ace.

You feel you've escaped his grip but get ready for the smear campaign comin' around the bend.

He doesn't have to skill set to come to grips with this so prepare for violence when his anger is lit.

How I do things, what I like, how I spend my time--it's all ME, ME, ME now and I'm in heaven, wow.

I felt I was being sucked dry--no one to talk to, no one cared if I lived or died. Destiny: bye bye.

Constantly feeling so violated with blurry boundaries--emotional and psychological treachery.

Toxin: The ongoing buildup of anger: tension, frustration and annoyance creates snappiness.

Snappiness against secondary objects shows a worn-out system, you've lost all distinctions.

HEALTH-DRAINING RELATIONSHIPS

Horrible relationships like this can only be endured in good health otherwise you'll get worse.

LOSERS and Femme Fatales

It was so gut wrenching and energy depleting I could only endure a bad marriage when young.

At this age I put my comfort and liberty first and wouldn't endure this for a minute sis.

Or if he's like that just allow him to pay the bills but you establish your separate life within walls.

To be under the same roof with a warring faction who hates your guts and busts your wants.

To have to endure and witness his crude, callous ways imposed on you by a barbarian, truly.

It was living with a black cloud and a gutsick feeling of nausea and fear every horrible moment.

LIVING WITH A RATTLESNAKE

It was like living with a rattlesnake, never knowing what the hell he'd do next, this little man fake.

I hated his guts, I prayed only to God, I made secret plans, He opened the route, it was done.

I will never adapt to little man again. For they are the worst for controllin' just to feel their manhood.

I could say nothing and he'd turn to me, fuming. I truly feared he'd push me outa the car soon.

Woman spends the second half of her life fuming and digesting the first half, were we all molested?

Before you can release with love you may have to release with hate but just lock that gate.

So sad: The worst he could do was lock me out--in the snow, along with my house-adapted cat.

LOSERS and Femme Fatales

Have nothing to do with a little man. You may think he's vulnerable so will stay in line, no chance.

I can feel the intense emotions now, of being sucked dry emotionally and discomfirmed by a clown.

These people are oblivious to you and anything you care about or stand for. Oblivious to the core.

You can't educate them, like style its inborn. You just have to be alone for awhile to be reburn.

You become increasingly less effective from built up emotions/stress, you codependency-regress.

I WAS NICE AFTER ALL

After I was free I realized I was a nice person after being told I was nothing, beaten down constantly.

Reconsider the time spent with that toxic person. See it as literal poison injected into you hon'

I can't afford to be with people who say "here, have some of my poison" and it's everywhere today.

I shudder thinking of all the people I've known like this. They were all liberals from California then.

They're purposely cruel, casually taking pot-shots just cuz they can. It's a pissing contest man.

He will never understand you, he can't understand you, he doesn't care to and you're nothing too.

That's just the way it is, nothing can be done about it, it's over, he doesn't have the skills, let go of.

REGAIN YOUR BOUNDARIES NOW

LOSERS and Femme Fatales

As you regain your healthy assertiveness, decisiveness and firmness you will win your highness.

I felt I was sucked dry, I cried day and night. Now it's the magic moment and everything's alright.

After escape prepare for backlash but God rewards your freedom dash, He doesn't want this.

Decide to have wholesomeness in your relationships. No more game like this with narcissists.

Decide to live non-toxic, as you now have pure ingredients/no toxins in the environment.

Most famous female writer of the 21st century wants to remain a mystery and that's how it will be.

LEFTIST OBLIVIOUS LOSERS

Youth are either holocaust deniers or too dumbed to know about it. Why has it been erased? Think about it.

Depop Agenda was big then went underground after WWII, naturally. Now it's big again: abortion clinics.

It is scary and dangerous how dumbed they are yet they call us dumb in need of tyrannical teachers.

The riots come from the rise of Antifa, the push of fake media narratives/advance of the criminal class.

They want "justice" but no justice against them when they act up. They are entitled, innocent, corrupt.

There must be enough presence of a stabilizing force to make it untenable to continue, of course.

PROTESTS AND LOOTING

LOSERS and Femme Fatales

Protests, looting and demolished banks in La Mesa CA, my little hometown--and national guard called out?

Ray got us outa there four years ago, he could sense California was a sinking ship. But La Mesa?

They act like blacks are massacred by whites and none of it's true. It's the opposite but it's unrevealed.

POLICE exist to protect the weak from the strong. They wanna defund em just as they take our guns.

Why are Americans surrendering to violent mobs? They're insecure and intimidated as if the left is God.

It's so humiliating watching you kiss their ass. Whoever taught you to bow before man/lick anyone's boots?

AGENDA: TO DESTROY SOCIETY

It's a radical agenda meant to destroy society cuz once you remove the police the weak are killed suddenly.

We gotta be ready cuz they're opening with violence but this is just the first wave--suburbs are next, ok?

What makes the left so crazy is they keep getting caught but never get into trouble/live in a bubble.

This isn't over, we've only just begun. They've crossed a giant line now, they'll be back, count on it hon'.

I'm waiting for you forever my handsome destiny. You're all I think about, it helps me get thru this tragedy.

The dumbed left doesn't see this violence as a GLOBAL THREAT and so they minimize/accept it.

Sell your city house man. It's worth two million now but in a week may be worthless--this is permanent!

LOSERS and Femme Fatales

Get outa the way man. Things change suddenly all thru history and now you gotta see what's happening.

Don't minimize what's happening like dullards all around you, napping. They'll minimize to the end, sadly.

Reason they don't tap down on Iran etc.: it would be racist if they did that-- think about it, we've had it.

WHEN THEY WAKE UP THEY WON'T BELIEVE IT

When they wake up they still don't believe it: It's cognitive dissonance--can't admit how foolish they were.

There is an ideology of collectivism as kids are taught they'll get it all free and they'll be the ruling elite.

This is no game and it's not going away. The destruction of society--storefronts etc--is becoming mundane.

The New Religion of the left is white guilt and hating themselves. They worship/bow to self-hate.

They run around lionizing any black person, period. It's truly disgusting but they can't admit it.

The appeasement we've been taught is about to be our destruction and it's all about the election.

"The heartbeat of racism is denial but it's anti-racist to confess"--so if we say we're NOT it's a "yes".

One sign of God's wrath is to be suddenly surrounded by strangers. We don't want this, we want ours.

THEY'RE AGING BABIES

A 60 year old man and grandfather talking dirty like that? Think of the evil influence of that elderly cat!

LOSERS and Femme Fatales

Are you gonna talk like that–F-TALK–when you're 70 or 80? Why not grow up now/show morality?

I know, you wanna get the admiration of the young crowd. But it makes you disgusting, dirty and loud.

Left loves violent rioting for same reason they want mass immigration of a large underclass for controlling.

Gotta KNOW God is with you even when you think He's not. He goes silent sometimes so your faith comes out.

I suddenly realized all my enemies from birth were not Christians. That explains everything about em.

After fasting 24 hours I felt the top of my head elongate–encephalization/longhead on the first day.

You're all over the place man. Like any narcissist there's no predicting your mood so I'll now disattend.

Stop chasing men thru their pages. For it hurts you anyway: if a narc he tries to make you jealous.

ADDICTED: EMPTY SHELLS

All addictions make people empty shells. Where they were bright/inventive/witty now they're little old bitties.

The answer that never illuminates, that response that never arrives, the lack of breaks: fasting changes fate.

It doesn't have to be a 30-day, don't get crazy. Just start easy, a 24-hour fast then note your victories.

If the narcissist ghosts you cuz he found better supply, say HURRAY cuz you're better without him, ok?

He knows you won't put up with his crap so goes to better supply who tolerates 'til she too says goodbye.

LOSERS and Femme Fatales

He deliberately pops your bubble for no reason. He's not even angry, it's just the narcissist person.

He deliberately makes you happy only to make you sad. It's not you, it's just the demonic way of the bad.

PROTECTION, PROVISION, EXPANSION

I'd give up on him for he'll hurt you again. You need stability in your life so you can EXPAND.

I guess I went thru all this so I could give you these books along with some tips. To that long life, RIP.

Like FLOTUS said she'd NEVER chase a man who didn't love her. We should all heed that for sure.

He may not be perfect but he gives me STABILITY and that's all I want: happy homelife/expansion.

Marriage is like a fence that protects/insulates me from all that crap out there. It was hellish for sure!

I can do my thing and no one can stop me cuz my husband is right next door ready to pounce on em.

I don't have to deal with male sexual innuendos etc cuz I'm a married woman and it's not happening.

Marriage is Absolute Freedom for the Female.

You shouldn't even be GOING to a man's page [let alone home] if you're married. Have true fidelity.

A woman should never let a man in her home alone. What will the neighbors think? It's very wrong.

MARRIAGE IS FREEDOM FOR FEMALES

All I had in life was human resistance but when married it was full throttle ahead, rid of obstructions!

LOSERS and Femme Fatales

Jesus said adultery starts in the MIND. You must push out thoughts of men outside your marriage bind.

A spouse may not have boldness to tell you she/he doesn't like you going to their pages, so I am today.

So I'm gonna assassinate you today by NOT going to your page in which case you are DEAD to me, hurray.

I fought people off ALL my life from bothering/pressuring me. In an instant when I said "I DO", I was free.

No one's messing with my military man Ray, so the lifelong sense of obstructions cleared suddenly.

BEHIND A FENCE YOU EXPAND!

If a woman wants to expand she's gotta be married so she CAN. Contrary to feminism, it's the only way man.

A single woman is a sitting duck, outa luck with no one to help her outa the muck and it's rough.

When single everyone tried to control me but when married it was like I was out of prison and finally free.

Sisters, mother, aunts, their friends, neighbors, busybodies, gossips ALL sought control of me.

Why go to his page if you know a narcissist will deliberately try to make you jealous? Resist!

For they are children who get off making you miserable--it gives them a definite thrill seeing you crumble.

Never be caught dead even thinking of a man like that. How would FLOTUS handle his ghosting crap?

If he uses sexual innuendo you must know you can't trust him. He crossed that line too soon the bum.

LOSERS and Femme Fatales

For you have had it with come here-go away relationships which destructively cycle through sex.

He obviously has a harem waiting in the wings if things go sour. Just this alone shows him as a player.

So goodbye, I guess I was wrong. I thought you were really up there inspired and glowing, but just a bum.

If there's something carnal/evil in you it comes across in your work and I don't wanna hear it jerk.

When they're all into their "blackness" it's gotta be suspicious, be an exemplar/human supremist.

First I feel sorry for you seeing your humanity. Then you rear up in total arrogance making me loony.

I want a man stable all the time, sorry. You can be ultra-creative but not this thing making me crazy.

NO MORE IDENTITY POLITICS!

Oh, they're into their blackness, their queerness or whatever. It's the biggest indicator, it's over.

I couldn't believe what evil children put me through. There are no lines, no decency, it's hellish too.

Saying NO to the devil makes the lust lure go away. Temptation thru history is always the same.

The fall of our culture being replaced by another who assumes it's superior/we've reason to fear.

If you wanna come out on top then take his last insult or ugly mistake and make it central, now GO.

I still have acid reflux but feel confident 60 hrs fasting weekly will reduce/eliminate it, it sux.

LOSERS and Femme Fatales

God put me in such pleasant circumstances to weather this out and it's like I'm being supplied from without.

The wide gulf/disparity between public education and true education is breaking up families as we speak.

EMOTIONAL INDOCTRINATIONS

The indoctrination is so emotional and intense on that childish level it reaches a violent crescendo.

I'm not gonna go there and be hurt by you again. I see now you're a sadist and this isn't love, yuk!

It's too hurtful to love you so I'm gonna stay with what I know. May not be exciting but our life's a ball.

They are mentally deficient bowing to others like a humiliated puppy when they did nothing really.

You're way outa my league baby with your player mentality and it comes thru strong, you need unreality.

As long as you go there he eclipses your own personality, don't you see that? The rejection is constant.

You hurt me so much and I don't have to say how. You sure didn't appreciate what God gave you now.

CURE FOR LOSERS: BECOME FASTERS

Any goat, cow, lizard, cat or dog can do it. Does that make you some great player? No, GROW UP!

It's been a great regimen I will continue for life: Fast every weekend 60 hours from Fri 6 pm to Mon 6 am.

It's a self-cleaning body so if we don't eat, 85% of our energy [for digestion] goes to detox instantly.

LOSERS and Femme Fatales

If you must take something, a little yellow fruit juice auto-digests the gut residue: lemon or pineapple.

From Friday pm to Monday am: fasting is easy and seen correctly it's a exhilarating/adventurous reality.

I have so much energy on my weekend fasts I generally tear into housecleaning, ordering closets, projects.

I figured I was never hungry anyway and besides cooking is a chore, so why not fast? Found time, galore.

It's like encephalization is the reward for enduring hunger pain. It just lasts a minute before giant gains.

Started my fast 4pm Friday then worked all night long ordering a huge basement without sleep, ok?

You just gotta say: I WILL endure hunger pain, it ain't no big thing, it's no sweat, I'm higher than that.

EATING BECOMES IRRELEVANT/A CHORE

With women it's too much about hair. We have enough on our plate, I recommend head coverings/flare.

LOSERS and Femme Fatales

They keep head warm, they top me off. That's what dad said--in his day everyone wore hats or turnoff.

I love my 1/16" buzzcut but not criticism from Christians like JLP so I wear head coverings and it's all ok.

You will reach an age where eating is irrelevant to you, even the good stuff cuz digestive pain is rough.

I don't like it, I'd rather be high as a kite with ALL THAT ENERGY now going to my higher poetic mind.

I WILL endure hunger pain. For I know restriction in respect to a principal brings BLISS always/again.

As a youth I always fasted on Sundays to feel closer to the Lord. Even missing church I had a reward.

I always knew if I had a test or a chore the next day, fasting on the previous made it a cakewalk/high pay.

Everything works with ease and alacrity: you become well oiled you might say. Coordination, elasticity.

Eat 4 days, fast 3 days: that's my version of the Snake Diet. A two-speed life: weekends vs weeks.

WE'RE WOUNDED CHILDREN

He got angry at the camera/threw it on the floor, ruining it even more--aging babies everywhere.

It's no sin to be tempted. We're all tempted, Jesus was tempted but we don't give in or it's repented.

Common with men: prostate cancer then impotence. They try to repair it thru porn but it makes it worse.

It's VERY common with men: trying to repair impotence with porn but they end up losing wife and home.

LOSERS and Femme Fatales

Once a wife discovers porn she may forgive/forget but it comes back--the deep dark horror of smut.

Whenever you find yourself running after "him" it's a sign of an inner wound needing your attention.

Trying to become whole thru another person who evokes those trauma chemicals seeking correction.

When I think of you I think of sexual innuendos or blatant outright sexuals and it's very bad ya' know.

Sexual trends take over the herd and it's debauchery. Just do things the old fashioned way.

Social Psychology--the Herd--is a scary thing when you see how unmanageable it is destroying everything.

Another way of being victimized is to be forgotten. We should learn of the holocaust then go on.

They're so dam dumbed and dangerous I'm glad I got away fast. Four years now safety from mobs, at last.

FENCED OFF FROM THE MOB

If you're not fenced in the mob will come right in on you--once they enter your house you're screwed.

The leftist mob thinks nothing of your private property or ownership--it's all theirs just cuz they want it.

A country neighborhood way WAY out and how I love it. Rooster in morning, aft breeze, crickets, stars.

Way out from HERDS: they'd have to cross the Grand Canyon to find me, this is MAXIMUM safety.

Antifa is the enforcement arm of the democrat party. This is their last stand after their other treacheries.

LOSERS and Femme Fatales

We know Bill Clinton wanted to use the military to cause civil unrest, Martial law and gun confiscation.

GO EMPTY SO GOD WILL FILL

When you become empty, prepare to be filled. For nature abhors a vacuum so just wait, prepare, be still.

The more empty the more filled you will be. Just when most would feel panic you see the signs of victory.

You see lackluster snobs gaining riches/fame by playing the game. Do you give up as socially lame? NO WAY

You see silly fools gaining acclaim cuz the peanut gallery's so inane. Look up, your victory is today.

Yes, no one pays any attention to you. That's the way it is in dense generations but God is cool and He rules.

MY OWN BORDERS

"Biblical Proportions": The fall of a city, the fall of a wall when the hordes come in.

Casual drop-ins are a curse. The devil sends distractions, cares and anxieties to steal the word. Mark 4: 19

I suddenly saw: that every problem I had came from wanting solitude while being bugged by the rude.

Even the churches acted like I didn't have a right to be alone! They bored me, I wanted solitude (the throne).

They see the social world as a religion--worshipping THEM. They hate you cuz you're independent.

I would go deep inside to a tranquil abundant garden, only to be yanked to the surface into total boredom.

LOSERS and Femme Fatales

To think the liberal worldview held us bound for 50 years, walking on eggs and causing our tears.

Parents across America are dealing with this: having to succumb to their devilish kids out of fear of reprisal.

She appeals to the herd who is just like her. But is that genius? No way, you have to mis-fit to have allure.

I was so happy and serene then my liberal sister started up with all this crap--a black cloud scene.

All of a sudden there was all this stuff we had to deal with--far-fetched, made up, demonic, saddening.

DISTRACTIONS VS. SOLITUDE

Right when I'm learning something about God or the deeper meanings to a verse, I am distracted.

EVERY problem had the same basis: the conflict between wanting solitude and dealing with the dudes.

Feminist women are the worst. Think a "feminist" would be nice to other women? The shrews are cursed.

Blowback: the unintended adverse results of a political action or situation. See: Streisand Effect.

The socially-hypotized took my desire for solitude as an INSULT--an affront to them. I coulda been killed.

How could I explain to a buncha dummies that "I'm a genius, I must be alone to work"--I felt cursed.

And they can't stand correction, crying or fighting back--they go to their cronies and you're in trouble Mack.

It's the Dunning-Kruger effect that the dumb think they're smart and they've an echo chamber of dark hearts.

LOSERS and Femme Fatales

Cuz kids get violent--that's their conflict resolution. Parents give in to keep peace, what else can they do.

Their evil knows no bounds, all you can do is stay away. They are compelled to low actions so avoid em, ok?

The dumb think they're smart and can't stand correction (gather an army) so we succumb to this tragedy.

The dumb are cruel, without restraint. The scary thing here is we're controlled by brute strength.

The terror of systems grouping against me created such implosion I felt compelled to write it all down.

In times of disorder people are cruel and negligent. From this stems social psychiatry or Systems Theory.

They turn what was a normal life into an upside-down, evil life. All cuz Satan said she was a lesbian/a lie.

GENIUS DOESN'T FIT, CHAMELEONS AREN'T LEGIT

You can't be a genius and fit in. That's just a way of making money but against evil you're not rebellin'

She wants to be seen as a great writer/genius but she's just like em--hammering same talking points, fakin'

She repeats same talking points and CHANGES with em. All for popularity--she's no genius just faking it.

She makes it ALL about her. If she has a great life she says they can all have it too, SHE is the magic cure.

Every detail of her magical life she makes accessible to the world since she's the center, what a girl.

But when things go wrong she becomes a ruthless enemy and balances forces by creating tragedies.

LOSERS and Femme Fatales

Only the woman who can transcend self will go down in history as the magic elf. A discoverer making y'all well.

Her book is based on a false premise: that there is no God after all--she's even embarrassed she was involved.

So we're supposed to leave religion and join Danuta in her winery with her new rich husband she found?

The mark of the Jezebel Spirit is how she'll rise up against you given the chance. She takes over, the witch.

She fights by getting an army against you. All her Johns or go-fers will target you and even torture.

Her tweets NOT intended to edify but rather ANNOUNCE events all about her--nothing to learn here!

Women just can't seem to get beyond their selves unless they become a pure saint with moral restraints.

That's where they give themselves away: liberal talking points reveal them as debauched witches, ok?

Since she's a popular fit-in (just like them) she's not as assiduous on details, like her looks: not a perfectionist.

POPULAR APPROVAL SEALS THEIR DEMISE

Hey broad, you get popular approval of feminist witches but look like an amoral pagan fool to the rest of us!

Having spent three decades in the wilderness I can spot em in a minute: the female culture conformists.

To be spouting female-friendly crap like that and feeling superior doing so-- that's not my map, gotta go.

The Jezebel will get her army against you and suddenly you're the minority. Now you're in trouble, truly.

LOSERS and Femme Fatales

If successful she can't see how it's all about her. God help us, bring her down before we're dead/it's over.

She's famous/married a rich man so now you can all do the same cuz she's the new template: what a dame.

She's the new evangelism: you can be like HER. There is no God otherwise just a utopian future.

If she gets enough disciples--satellite fan club--it's an echo chamber and her ego grows even more.

She married a rich man and her life became magical so yours can too--just by believing, that's so cool.

Ok, you can see who she is and how she will bring herself down, now resume your work, be renowned.

The more empty, the more filled. The more zero, the more massive. The more ignored, the more attractive.

NOT the point that she's a debauched backstabbing witch but that you ever got involved in the first place.

RUTHLESS GOSSIPS AND TALEBARERS

Most women know nothing but shout silly slogans. And you husband cuckholds actually defer to THEM?

Angry feminist culture is based on two fundamental things: virtue signaling and people-worshipping.

When a man can't state his opinions without looking at his wife first I have to say it's totally disgusting.

People-worship (not God worship) is cruel. Those they respect they cow-tow to and those below they pooh.

Taught to be "loving" they speak of others in glowing terms while marginals are caught in old webs/spurned.

LOSERS and Femme Fatales

Men duke it out but with women, what else she got? Her tongue--subtle sly sadistic lies, half-truths, slander.

My own mother, my own sisters--talking about me that way to the neighbors! Even perfect strangers.

There is NO loyalty with these sleazy liberal feminists. They don't know the first thing about it, social fascists.

It's all about ostracism from clique or clan. That little genius is the odd girl out and they hate her, man.

The way they think is purely insanity-making. Especially if the victim is a genius yet not yet self-realized.

As the men couldn't control me the women hated me cuz I wouldn't conform, I was just like Thee.

The true psychiatry is Social Psychology as systems create personality as mal-adaptations to tragedy.

She virtue signals on trendy topics she knows nothing about but as an accepted narrative she feels supported.

You can't argue with a Jezebel like that cuz "everyone knows" she's right tho' these ideas are a blight.

Since women are taught to view themselves thru the eyes of others, approval not truth is all that matters.

CREATE A SPACE: BYE-BYE BABY

Say No so you can say Yes to the important. "Successful people say no to everything." Warren Buffet

Saying "NO!" creates space for what is important to us. Say NO to stop busyness, which is dryness.

"NO" is the most important word in our vocabulary. All problems come from saying "YES", truly.

LOSERS and Femme Fatales

Because of who you let in to your life you have no one to blame but yourself for all that anguish and strife.

We need men to protect us but what gives as they become beta males terrified of their wives and their B.S.?

Failing media links with Silicon Valley to ban competitors as "hateful" when they are the ones, despicable!

It's literally: Where do they get their news--that's what it all comes down to! A total brainwash too.

DEMONIC FORCES IN POLITIX

Demonic forces always wear a loving facade. It's the wolf in sheep's clothing: it's chic, joyous, mod.

How far we've slid: It's now ok to say assaulting someone is LESS a crime than calling a man a "man".

Femmes: If a baby killer I don't wanna hear you talking about love, sacrifice or your selfish "rights".

No, we don't have to respect Merkel/Mae just cuz they held office--they opened their countries' floodgates!

Britain is a nation of sleeping lions, best not to wake em up--guess what, Mae's gone/they're woken up.

Why respect Merkel/Mae cuz they held office? They both ruined their countries, flooding em with hostiles.

If anyone needs 'time out,' it's Pelosi, who abandoned the party of JFK to the party of AOC.   Laura Ingraham

Dear Lord, please increase this domino effect as people wakeup to the horror of late term abortion.

To the past in Borrego: I do not know you, you swindling festering demons.

LOSERS and Femme Fatales

The further you are in Christ the less impressed with people--but the less you grow the more they're real.

There are demons covering whole neighborhoods, cities and states. Put it all in a bag, throw it out/escape.

When you squirm over past events, go meta: put it ALL in a bag to forget now just focus on lost America.

There are demons controlling towns so put all that happened in a bag then throw the dam thing out.

NOXIOUS EVENTS ARE JUST TRAINING

All those noxious embarrassing events were just your training so nothing like that ever happens again.

You had to go through it, look at it like that. Just the fact you're in that situation meant you were still a brat.

The thing distinguishing winners is they don't let the past control em and each day's is new like beginners.

It's such a big thing that Paul's entire goal was to leave the past behind for it's really: destiny or tragedy?

Even before it happened I felt guilt and shame--it was inlaid by the sick systems I mal-adapted to, ill-famed.

If you're a child of God do you think He'd leave your past besmirched? He erases when you were cursed.

Successful people say NO to everything. Unless given good breaks or money which is the whole thing.

Most people only know the size of Kim Kardashian's behind not who Napoleon was. Michael Savage.

I loved how Trump went after Mayor Khan. He's a thorn in our side and those lines need be drawn.

LOSERS and Femme Fatales

Concepts like "climate change" are pushed so intensely they gain a life of their own in a hypnotized society.

People are controlling. Unless you're on top it's best to stay away in your own reality so liberating.

It took a lifetime to be alone to think and write. It's like you won't get it unless you achieve it as a right.

If you're a woman they won't leave you alone until you're an old crone and only then your life is your own.

The world is loud, chaotic, meaningless, gibberish, egoistic, sensual, devilish: I just want God and myself.

HYPERSEXUALIZED TEEN WORLD

The hypersexualized teen world is a hellish den a young girl enters. Hell only knows what happens afters.

How's she supposed to adapt? Being Miss Priss will get her attacked. Few young women can resist: fact.

Eldering, or sagacity, is mining the past for pearls of wisdom. Seeing events in different ways as you wizen.

It is so relieving as old resentments reconstellate into new views and we are free: that's eldering to me.

It's a loud, social, meaningless, egotistic, showy, nonsensical, arrogant world. Reject or be under its curse.

They are intentionally disgusting and overbearing. I want peace and separation from the unforgiving.

If you're finicky and orderly they'll purposely mess you up. They'll use up all your time for their stuff.

Don't let em in/don't get in their car. Never be at their mercy even for a minute cuz they'll start a war.

LOSERS and Femme Fatales

The old movies are so much better where they don't rely on SEX or EFFECTS which are puerile or hellish.

I just don't do groups anymore, in this generation they are mean and uppity even Calvinists can be.

What is the joy of retirement? Not having to put up with em anymore--NO one, we've closed those doors.

Fake church virtue signals global homocultural motifs as God becomes a maleable trope, interchangeable, fluid.

They have replaced Christian customs with an exotic operational framework of postmodern sloganism.

LIBERAL NIGHTMARE: SELECTIVE BLINDNESS

Liberal nightmare: selective blindness as we compare the image they project with the dark reality behind it.

Right vs left: Reason and decency vs. lunacy and chaos.

You're at the stage now where you've gotta stay apart. Not only are you known they'll break your heart.

CNN pays people to hate Trump and talk about it. I'm a little surprised at some of em though, the twits.

If you're too accessible they'll make your life miserable and I don't mean maybe they need you baby.

It's the cantankerous callousness, they can't help making a mess and it freaks out the oldsters I guess.

I try to cleanse my memory by looking at beautiful pictures of the desert instead of all the evil social spirits.

Even churches confronted me for wanting to be alone. That's the true religious experience and throne.

LOSERS and Femme Fatales

Forget the creepy events in the desert experience and take in the WHOLE: you are complete, yourself.

To the creepy emergent church, social equals religious. It's all about acceptance not God I guess.

SOCIAL DOESN'T MEAN RELIGIOUS

The democrats say: send mass illegals to red cities, don't send em to us—and they're gonna pay for it.

The emergent church (we're all "one"): Their church is fake and they are fake Christians hon'

"Life depends on compromise"--not when it means loss of our sovereignty to the rabble, these are lies.

How fascinating: Every bad experience became a chapter in my books on Abnormal Psychology, ole.

See time collapsed: each bad event is a jigsaw-puzzle fit which becomes something very legit.

But now it's all over, God took out the interlopers and I'm behind a fence and locked gate forever.

I more than anyone else knows what it's like with open borders cuz I was invaded by a buncha losers.

They make up terms to make the new reality real.

It's far more convenient to stay married especially in a country torn by internal wars which bring misery.

How vanity + ego + low IQ has led to the funeral of original thought. Michael Savage

Today I will talk about sin. We all did crazy things under it's influence, that's why we have to forgive em.

LOSERS and Femme Fatales

Biblically, "perfect" doesn't mean without error, fault or blemish but ripe, mature, ready, complete, whole.

Every warrior deserves rest and reward. Would-be genius has an incapacity for leisure but not me Lord.

EMERGENT CHURCH COMFORTS SINNERS

Not the new BS of comforting the sinner but instead showing him the results of sin which is disaster.

They're just suspicious of everything we do. Every conservative knows what it's like to be pigeonholed.

We are pegged, outlawed, scapegoated by the liberal crowd. They never give up pushing our face in the mud!

Just a friendly reminder: You are here now not there pal. It was awful I know but how else: you now?

There's no reason to take it personally unless you're a fat messy housekeeper or a liberal feminist loser.

You jumped on my gravy train and drove it straight into the mud. It was pure chaos not just what I lost.

MEMORY STORED IN SHIT

Old toxins go out thru bloodstream and you're now in the pits. Don't forget, memory's stored in shit.

Addiction: Trying to get pleasure in a sea of brokenness and anguish. We're washed up tho' it's passed.

With the heart of God you see the nations different--you see situations and people as dull or aberrant.

It's not that I don't wanna be with you but life is a pie. The most important is God's work for which I'd die.

LOSERS and Femme Fatales

Yes God put it in me long ago. This work is magnificent but not to you below but I don't care, ya know.

So you don't see it--that's ok with me. I'll go to my grave doing it cuz the Lord put it into me, you see?

The more explosively magnificent your future the less will be happening now, a good thing to know.

People are cruel so unsub discussions for now. God judges the heart not futile debates with lowbrows.

With depression or fatigue ask: who (have i been around) or what (have i attended to)--a daily task.

Music mutes bad thoughts while opening up new revelations--settling doubts and untying knots.

THEY EFFECT US LIKE DOWNERS

She affected me like a pill or downer. I wanted to sleep for days, I felt sick at heart, I wanted my momma.

I'm taking a break from news. It's keeping me from thoughts of heaven, God, my cosmic mind cruise.

You love wifey though she believes in killing babies, lesbian affairs with neighbor ladies or being shady?

The home must shirk evil and be thorough. Don't allow dirty jokes or the house becomes dirty with sorrow.

Sin affects your aura too. A glowing saint from within or muddy colors like mauve, drab, black and blue.

Thus the final reason for repentance for would-be saints was the desire for beauty and not by chance.

He affected me like a pill. I wanted to escape, cry, die--that's the effect of Satan who comes to steal or kill.

LOSERS and Femme Fatales

If you're going through a storm but have a revelation of its purpose you can still have joy and be earnest.

It's contact = conquest. NO contact means no mess or the energy drains right out of God's kids/His best.

They'll tell you what to think whether you want it or not. They'll impose their advice tho' its pure rot.

Every time democrats talk I wanna vote twice: the debauchery, the cruelty, the machinations, the vice.

Is anyone really good and nice? Even Lord Jesus said "don't call Me good, only God is"--that's right!

HYPERSENSITIVES READ THOUGHTS: OUCH

The hypersensitive reads everyone's thoughts: gestures, inflections, raised eyebrows, lies they bought.

I was miserable in liberal environments and you creeps will never see me again cuz I'm a social scientist.

How could you agree with liberals, dark heart? Tho' it's just for approval you're supposed to be set apart!

Holy means separate--you're NOT a part of the herd. They are dull conformists and people-worshippers.

They are sick, evil, can't hear and don't care. Demons own their mind and they are ordinary/without flair.

The devil extracts the panache right outa you. You had style, flair, audacity but now just a screaming shrew.

Seeing the system surrounding pathology is not like blaming others but understanding the reason.

The system of wrong thoughts created an environment I wanted only to escape but in it I was distraught.

LOSERS and Femme Fatales

Don't be a dam beta male. How can men defend us if they're afraid of women and their wives--do tell!

Emotional cut-offs [NO CONTACT] means no symptoms. That's the way it works, see it as a system.

When everyone hates you for your thoughts while hammering lies they bought you're tired and distraught.

They say geographical relocation won't help but I disagree: it changes neurons and bad feelings you felt.

If you wanna see me come on my turf where I'm set up, not me going on yours where you've messed up.

I thought he was a great preacher 'til he said God wanted open borders--you abused podium for politics sir.

DELAY BETWEEN PLANTING AND HARVESTING

There's a natural delay between planting and harvesting--waiting is part of the game so keep maturing.

You never plant and harvest in the same season--there's a time for everything so look forward in anticipation.

Waiting is always a test. It tests your character, your trust, your faith and endurance--just EXPECT.

WAITING is the problem with everyone and it's definite--it's when God watches how you'll handle it.

It's a people-worshipping generation. Resist this cuz it's people not God and that is idolatry/unAmerican.

If you talk against people they hate you but if they talk against God it's ok in a nation of losers/fools.

They act like PEOPLE are God. Well they ain't--most are going to hell and about God couldn't care less.

LOSERS and Femme Fatales

They are brainwashed globalist armies not victimized third world populations and its the United Nations.

Don't worry about your detractors: they are setup to fail and will bring themselves down.

Are they scared of their wives or fear being deprived?

A shove-down since the sixties is "we're all one": A Hitler is the same as a saint--that's the silly lesson.

Get a grip--we're not all "ONE". Separate yourself from the mob of debauched sin-justifiers--that's "love".

They're so poorly educated they can't grasp depth or concepts--the Millennials just shout old narratives.

What do you mean "in your day"--what a thing to say! My day is NOW callous ageist, go away.

LIONS REJECT OPINIONS OF SHEEP

A lion never loses sleep over the opinions of sheep. Champions and great thinkers Old Saying

Let sleeping dogs lie. Don't go back--just think of the things you did when young, lax, prickly as tacks.

Father thank you for Your word that washes me, cleanses me, inspires me, heals me and delivers me.

When you give me Your wisdom in heals me of all affliction and inoculates me against persecution.

I loved how Trump went after Mayor Khan. He's a thorn in our side and those lines need be drawn.

If I want it to be true it MUST be true said the 4-year old. I'm the center of my universe, tell me I'm good.

LOSERS and Femme Fatales

Climate Change Hysteria is just another redistribution scheme. Pay them a buncha money and you'll be free.

The Green New Deal is just a sales pitch for socialism. Putting "green" in front of anything acts like hypnotism.

Women are brittle when it comes to criticism so want censorship but it's ok for them to have angry fits.

Just do your great work then let it stand on its own. You're above insulting interviews--why should you?

They feel invincible then start to slip then double down which greases the skids in their expressway to hell.

CAPTURED LEFTIST CHURCHES

Captured, leftist-run churches rent out rooms to drag queen child rapists so they can capture your children.

With these drag queen incursions into the schools they are testing the perch with your children--don't be fools.

Methodists are like re-education camp: there are not two genders, global Islam is good, families are bad.

The bodies of the zombies begin to break down having been taken over by demons urging bad acts.

When taken over by demonic spirits the real person is gone, after being overwritten by new program.

An informed upwardly-mobile population stands in the way of globalists--they want us dumb messes.

A woman in deep sin will also let sinners in. That's how it is when her hedge is down and fools abound.

Any woman concerned with women's rights should be concerned with Islam but the left embraces it ma'am.

LOSERS and Femme Fatales

We need to reversal diet. The minute I switch from news to music and Bonanza I'm simply exhilarated.

Talking videos made chaos in my brain. That's what I sacrificed to get the info but now I'm done, just sayin'.

Cuz with music or beauty it opens MY brain MY reality MY destiny and it's always better than you honey.

All it did was make me bitter and sad. Even conservative news showed me clips of what the left guys said.

What creates the great patriots? Those with the IQ to feel deep in their soul for their historical ROOTS.

Every minute I spend in music or looking out the window is money in the bank and bringing destiny out.

FASCINATION OF YOUR OWN MIND

Nothing's as good or fascinating as your own mind. Develop good ground for that and avoid the blind.

Though seems like decades of dung--the silent years--it was fertile anarchy occurring underground/tears.

I must have been so wild that God HAD to put me through all that. It was so extreme, the Potter's slap.

I fought for the right to be alone and won. I overcame the social undertow, a recluse ya know—it's fun.

It is most profitable to just look out the window.

My time is limited, I wanna explore the infinite. Can't miss a minute as it's all designed and luscious.

If you don't wanna hurt workers and poor people you don't bring in foreigners to compete for their jobs: duh!

LOSERS and Femme Fatales

Third world immigrants drive down wages, obviously--it's always big business behind this travesty.

Those who favor unrestricted immigration care nothing for the people whose standard of living vanishes.

Arkancides abound and the reason is never found.

Claim you're fighting racism, keep your party in power and let the workers rot--that's the American left.

She really wanted her family to come around but eventually just gave up cuz they were too far gone.

PUNISHED BY THEIR PRESENCE

Yay I never have to be punished by your presence again. I've learned my lesson and am now well-fenced in.

With me being that dumb and wishy-washy they were compelled to test the perch in this awful tragedy.

They're making their move after years of writing about it. Since the 60's they've hated America you twits.

To become big, be nothing. Your problem is thinking you're something but to God be the glory, He's king.

It is so relieving to become nothing and not have to contend or stress out over this thing cuz God is working.

I need more time with my own family: husband, dogs and cats. Now God will take care of the rest.

I'm sick of news, too depressing. I know it all: we're crashing/burning but let Trump do the worrying.

There's no more I can say: we're being intentionally replaced.

Satan is the author of bad thoughts coming to mind, so don't choose them as they come streaming by.

LOSERS and Femme Fatales

God wants you to be happy in good (overcoming, victorious) thoughts--so you know these are not.

While the culture went politically correct justice warriorship I was in a tiny desert cabin completely separate.

What is normal to them is preposterous to me. We're to coddle the "loving" humans filled with treachery.

Some are sleazy, ugly, fat or unfit, loudmouthed and obscene, filthy, covered in bad art, debauched and mean.

We're to prefer being with them rather than alone, as social transcends independence (our throne).

In fact preferring to be alone is snobbery to them. Who do you think you are, not hanging with "friends"?

In this social generation the RIGHT to be alone and independent is the most hard-won achievement.

I fought to be alone so I could think. For in their presence is chaos, ineptitude, wrong focus, rinky-dink.

SEEKING SOLITUDE CAN BE DANGEROUS

When you seek solitude--when the slave escapes the plantation--it isn't that easy as they get rude.

Come back into your situation: hear the wind, watch the cat, think and no more chat--that's where it's all at.

Because they feel guilty (ashamed too) they wanna FORCE us to see them in a good light, not eschew.

Rather than giving up loved sins they force us to say it's all-ok like God doesn't care where they've been.

Since when is "resisting Marxism" the same as white supremacy? Absurd but that is the way it'll be.

LOSERS and Femme Fatales

Now that you're mature don't get mad at the lessons bringing you here.

Be SUBTLE for the lack of subtlety turns competitors into enemies and enemies into fanatics. Jock Ewing

When He wants you a certain way, to serve a specific purpose on earth, it's a rigorous regiment for sure.

God wanted me to write about social fascism--ostracism in systems--so those were the hard lessons.

God had me on the Potter's wheel for three decades of torture! A boot camp of survival lessons for sure.

WOMEN CONTROL THROUGH GOSSIP AND OSTRACISM

I learned how women control their world through cruel gossip and ostracism-- that is the bully woman.

Female culture is conformist so when a unique genius arises they hate her, wanna kill/banish her.

Women turn on a dime when they hear contrary gossip--so socially inclined they can switch back/flip out.

She had me in constant fear of what she said to others about me. I knew she was doing it, the she bully.

Even mom and sisters gossiped about me shamelessly and without guilt--there was no loyalty with this ilk.

In times of chaos mothers turn against daughters and visa-versa: jealousy and soul murder in America.

You have interlocking jealousy patterns in sick families: Two against one-- either shifting alliances or none.

I was a bottomless pit of endless shame and guilt. A black hole inside and it was impossible to fill it.

LOSERS and Femme Fatales

Loved by my husband that horrible black cloud all went away. I feel secure and creative night and day.

With a good godly marriage every meal is a banquet and every day is a holiday to celebrate.

We hardly see each other but know they're there. Creative thinkers gotta be alone: it's holy and rare.

Without subtlety you'll be banned. You gotta be like a velvet glove, understated, humble, clever yet sly.

DANGEROUS HIX POLITIX

In California scarce resources are being lavished on illegal immigrants and the rest have to pay for it.

Climate change is a UN-led ruse to establish a New World Order.

Infants are not humans until you decide to keep them. Leftist ideology

We believe America should be a sanctuary for law-abiding Americans not criminal aliens. Donald Trump

The republicans: great jobs, safe neighborhoods, affordable health care, low taxes and secure borders.

The Democrats: mass migration, high taxes, high crime, late term abortion, infanticide, hoaxes/delusions.

Americana: We believe in the American farmer, worker, family and dream; the constitution and rule of law.

We believe in the dignity of work and the sanctity of life, that faith and family not government/bureaucracy.

We believe children be taught to love our country, our history--and always respect--dearly--our flag.

How to become big: become small.

LOSERS and Femme Fatales

The Jon Stewart thing was what liberals do: Show up later and take credit for other people have done.

The gratifications of the flesh are human nature without God. Walk in the spirit and they're gone.

This is a new theory in psychology: that all pathology comes down to Social Psychology.

Lessons God taught me about borders were horrendous but because He's there I know I won't ever repeat em.

JEZEBEL SPIRIT DESTROYS YOUR SELF WILL

I can spot em in a minute: female culture conformists or democrats putting illegals before Americans.

Alexandria Ocasio-Cortez: it's a reflection of the sick culture that she is so popular.

The Jezebel Spirit will rise up against you and destroy your self-will when given the chance (TAKE OVER).

Just say "that was a different era" then DON'T LET EM BACK IN. Seeing life in stages will stop em.

Canada is the weirdest "progressive" nation on the planet but Canadians daily ask: "What will he do next?"

It's extremely cruel for social media to hide the rules from us then retroactively issue punishments.

LADY PREACHERS

I love Joyce Meyers/Paula White even though everyone says they are heretics who love luxury.

I get a lot out of Joel Osteen tho' he rarely mentions Jesus. A motivational speaker, that's what he is.

LOSERS and Femme Fatales

If I keep my mind on Jesus I can know I'm holding to the highest possible thought, a captive of God.

Sometimes I see prevalent female neuroses coming thru women preachers and it gives me the creeps.

What happens when woman needs approval? Does this neurosis come through her loud preachin', pray tell?

What happens when the female pastor is mad at her husband, does this come through her preachin?

It's not that he keeps me happy but he keeps me afloat cuz I would always be happy anyway.

Male preachers tend to hold to the line more, females tend to make it all about them, it's just our nature.

She's a great preacher as long as her husband keeps her happy. "It's a matter of the anointing". Dave Meyers

AUTOIMMUNE DIET FOR THE SENSITIVE

Cooked food: brain grows/gut shrinks bc cooked auto-digests. Raw: gut grows to digest it as brain shrinks.

Intermittent Fast: 6 hour food window, 18 hours fasting daily. No sweat, I don't wanna eat again anyway.

By the time I've had smoothie-soup-salad I'm done for the whole day, I think I can still heal this way.

It's NOT heartburn, it's an immune reaction to wrong foods. Like an allergy to tomatoes, your major fuel.

It's NOT that you're terribly sick, ok? But that you're allergic to potatoes which you ate thrice a day.

Tomatoes are the biggest causes of leaky gut along with potatoes—both sustaining whole continents.

LOSERS and Femme Fatales

All of Mexico, Spain, Italy and the spud capitals Russia, Germany, Poland are sustained by nightshades.

Think of all the potatoes and tomatoes that go into everything! These are like staples, and yet worst to eat.

Whole continents living on potatoes--creates cultural psychology. Living on tomatoes: and pathology.

Who wants to eat all day long? That's what the vegans have to do and energetically it's low down.

The "Universal Cut" is 1/16" inch, not 1/8". It looks the best and is good for the fastidious who could care less.

I suppose if you're not allergic you can eat it, but the mere fact it puts holes in the gut=you're gonna show it.

I'm sick all the time unless I just stay home then I'm fine.

If allergic to tomatoes [nightshades] it's potatoes too--and all salad dressings with paprika, eschew.

Food taken daily becomes allergenic too. My staff for decades was avocados but now I am through.

Can't fast due to creature habits, inability to endure postponed gratification, wussies, slaves to tummy.

Medications (like antidepressants) bring lost charisma. They block the light and create opacity (paste on ya).

The vaccines don't protect you--they are scams. They are trojan horses for other disgusting things.

OLD LADY DIET: SMOOTHIES, SOUPS, SALAD, SALMON

SOUP: It's low in calories but high in nutrition and also satiety index. So you feel good/full and can fast.

LOSERS and Femme Fatales

Soup-eaters are always skinny. It's the little old lady diet: smoothies, soups, salads--nutritional density.

Smoothie: banana berry coconut kale parsley. Soups: veggies longcooked & pureed. Salads: as you please.

My one cheat is hazelnut-chocolate butter. It's so delicious I only pray it is good for me, but no matter!

My autoimmune protocol is not low-carb: smoothies, soups, salads & salmon then fast to tomorrow.

I'm a rasta vegetarian cuz I can't get protein from eggs or dairy restricted on the autoimmune protocol.

I can't eat land animals cuz I picture the animal. For some reason the fish is less so, and I need it ya' know.

NO TRIGGERED IMMUNE: FRUIT/SALADS

"No more triggered immune reactions by giving up grains, dairy, nightshades, citrus, seeds/nuts, eggs."

The inorganic fruit looks better usually. They chemicalize the way fruit looks while organic may look ugly.

In fact the better a fruit looks the less I'd trust it. It's too made-up, a food invention--don't eat it.

Just get whatever fruit and veggies are in season and make smoothies, soups, salads and have salmon.

Inorganic fruit is prettier cuz it's a chemicalized food invention. It's all skin deep and the effects are creepy.

She's really lost it, could be the medications after being pregnant. Don't let it, you can get it all back.

When the houseclean: when it needs it and you know I'll see it. If neat don't have to worry about it.

LOSERS and Femme Fatales

VICTORY IN DARKNESS: THIS BJ THING

There are times in history when sexual perversion takes off--a pandemic, doin' it in the streets--and God hates it.

You can spot em immediately--it's a great gulf between evil and good--and these are your enemies.

It is wrong for you to implant this BJ thing in the minds of husbands as if their wives are the problem!

To Mr. Deep Throat: Shut the f--- up. You're not a preacher nor a moral leader just a grunt.

Most wives don't like it, they just put up with it but the problem is the "forever contract": YUK!

TWO-SPEED LIFE: TUNNEL-VISION VS. RELAX

Work is tunnel-vision, screening out insights. Relaxation however opens it all up and the answer alights.

Although we started our weekend on Wednesday we still accomplish one good thing on our list daily.

Ten bird feeders on property and I gotta refill em daily. The amount they eat is amazing, I'll keep it coming.

How to evoke thought: put on music. Look out window. Pet cats. Such things are the most profitable.

I figured out where to go, I did it, I'm the home-maker and you're just the benefitter but that's ok mister.

I'm willing to wait to benefit you with all I have but if you're that dumbed ok I'll continue to wait/party all day.

Ancestors: if teetotalers they were great/famous orators but if they drank at all they died in the gutter.

DEEP THROAT AND THE ENDLESS CONTRACT

LOSERS and Femme Fatales

The new BJ Forever Contract means she's gotta demean herself on a daily basis. Women: WAKE UP!

How un-Queenlike to demean yourself like that just to please his weird fantasies! Wake up ladies!

It chokes me, it strangles me, I can't wait til it's over. That's what the ladies ALL said about deep throat fervor.

One time is never enough, it's gotta be a constant thing--are you kidding me? It's so humiliating.

I'd rather die then live like that--someone's live-in whore. Nothing is worth living like that in the gutter.

That's what men want--does that justify going to whores if his wife is disgusted and abhors it?

It's an apparent trend now. Does that mean the nice girls are now the bad guys you don't wanna know?

I'm an expert at leisure. I start my weekends on Tuesdays or earlier and that just releases work fervor.

LEISURE EVOKES GENIUS

You can never go wrong with leisure. But that's when you're hyper-creative too so prepare for work.

The would-be genius has incapacity for leisure--he can't relax without getting drunk or something similar.

WHENEVER you take the day off {mentally or whatever] the answer instantly arrives and it's so clever.

How to work/succeed: keep taking the day off/clearing the desk, keep starting a vacation now be blessed.

Don't keep forcing the fit, that's how work makes Johnny a dull boy. With Holy Spirit Ease it's done, ole.

LOSERS and Femme Fatales

WATCH OUT FOR WOMEN

The way women fight foes is to get others against em. They connect, do footwork, call em again.

Women ingather an army against you. They spill the beans to their friends, even speak in Al-Anon about you.

For your wicked slandering of me, the wicked in you was exposed. Everything comes back, ya know.

BIG SALAD religion: A little bit of Buddha, some Muslim, fold in Hindu now everyone will love ya too.

To constrain to pure doctrine is to make em mad. Their freedom is BIG SALAD religion and that's that.

They're not brought together by what they believe but how they feel--and if you don't feel it you're a heel.

The day I was Born Again I'll never forget. The God above got me out of Darwinism, just like that.

"Ecumenicism": one-world religion, we're all in it together, Christ is no different from the rest of em.

Suffering leads to endurance, endurance to character and character to hope. Paul

"Outer darkness" is how hell used to be preached. "Cut your hand off" to not go there Jesus beseeched.

BIG EGOS GOTTA GO

To God be the glory. Let him increase as we decrease and when small enough He'll give us the Victory.

There are no "Christians on the Left" despite justice warriors in the church bringing its swing to daft.

LOSERS and Femme Fatales

Any professor who is not far left is walking around scared to death. Heather MacDonald

Western Civilization is the source of liberty, freedom and extraordinary accomplishment.

100 KAREN KELLOCK BOOKS

AFFINITY OR MISERY
AGELESS CORNUCOPIA
AMERICA AWAKE!
AMERICA'S DAFT ERA
ARTS OF PALEO FASTING
AUTOPHAGY ON CHEATERS
BACKSTABBING NEUROTICS
BETRAYAL TRAUMA
BOOMERS AND BROKENNESS
BOOT ON NECK
CHAMPION GUIDES
COMMIE NUTHOUSE
COMMIES
COMMUNIST SPIRIT
CONTAGION OF MADNESS
CONTAGIOUS MADNESS
CULTURE CLASH BASHED
DAFT LEFT
DAILY FASTARIAN
DAM RATS
DIVERSITY IS CRUELTY
E-RACE WHITE
EVIL FREAKS (Beyond Gross)
THE END OR A BEND?
FEMALE BULLIES AND FEMI-NAZIS
FEMALE CARNALITY
FEMALE DUMB DOWN
FEMALE POWER DRIVE
FEMINISM AND RUIN 1 & 2
FIX FOR MISFITS
FOOLS & TRAMPS
FREEDOM SPEAKING
FRENEMY ENABLER
FRENEMY LIAR
FRENEMY THIEF
FRENEMY TRAITOR
TRENEMY TYRANT
GENIUS IS HELD DOWN
GLOBALISLAM
GOD USES THE FLAWED
HAZE OF THE LATTER DAYS

AUTHOR BIO

Karen Kellock Ph.D.

Ph.D Political Psychology, UCI 1976
Post-Doctoral: UCI Medical School
Department of Psychiatry
Grants NIMH, NIAAA

Ph.D. dissertation "A Systems-Theoretic View of Pathologic Interaction" made an early mark as the "Wife of the Alcoholic Syndrome". Postdoctoral research at UCI Medical, Dept. of Psychiatry on the systems surrounding pathology on NIMH and NIAAA federal grants: The Contagion of Madness: The Psychology of Neurotic Interaction and Pathological Systems. Therapy tool Therapeutic Playwriting introduced the play Mary and Murv: Gruesome Twosomes in the Alcoholic Marriage. She taught Abnormal Psychology and Pathological Systems Theory at UC and CSU campuses and developed "the Debris Theory of Disease" in 100 books and website: (www.karenkellock.org).